WILD THINGS ARE GOING TO HAPPEN

by Henrik Schrat

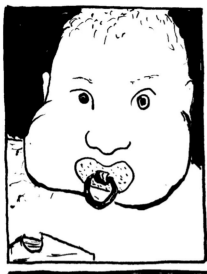

Like Le Corbusier... You see a direct lineage here?

Well that's what my friend Brian Hatton says. He was a Russian constructivist, he was from Georgia, and then he met Le Corbusier in **Paris**. So it's a merger of both of those styles. But of course my work because it comes out of Flavin and LeWitt, comes directly from **Russian Constructivism**. And a lot of my work is quasi-functional. My Waterloo Sunset at the Hayward Gallery is **quasi-functional**. The Dia Foundation piece has a video-take coffee bar, and I think Flavin's work is of course quasi-functional it's decoration, it's the illumination of the space and it's also art.

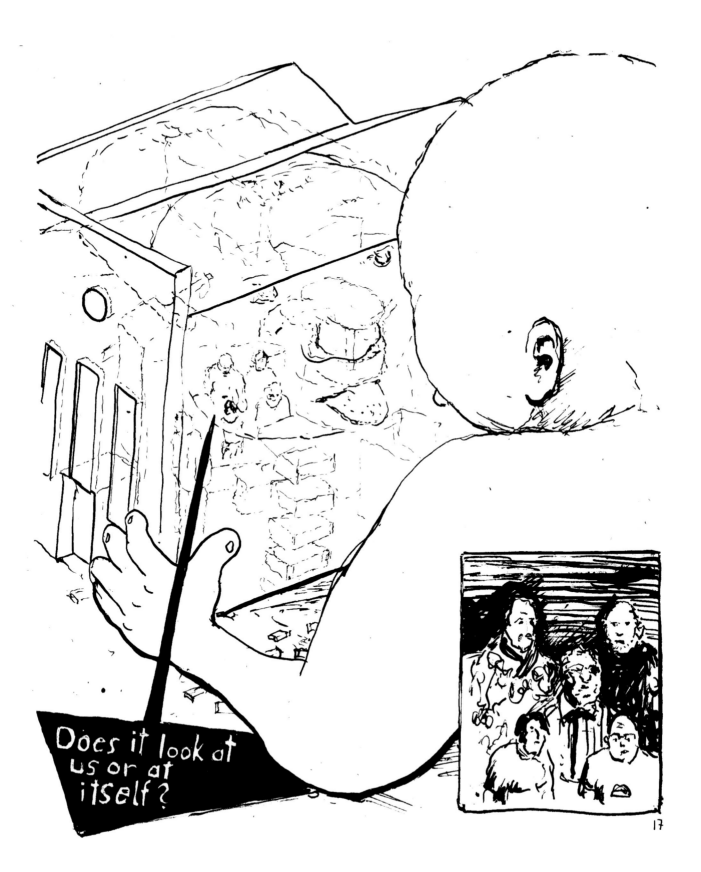

But yours is more confrontational in a way than Flavin's because I think, that's why it's influenced so many artists, actually ☺ because of that dealing with the functional and the non-functional at the same time, putting them ~~together~~

Well my work is always a **hybrid**, this work is a hybrid between art and architecture, my earliest work was a hybrid between **magazines** and what became conceptual art and **critical essays**.

Like "Homes for Amerika," like that series...

That was because you were finding a space that wasn't being used, did you see that you could populate that space and make art there, because nobody else was?

Of course you are correct... Also because the magazine page piece came about because I had a gallery and we showed **Sol LeWitt** and some early people who became minimal artists later. And the fantasy, the year that I had the show was, **to destroy value**.

Flavin put one of my shows on the floor of an opening of fluorescent light **and on the opening** someone stepped on the fluorescent lights — **they exploded** — he was very happy. He said his fluorescent lights should go back to the hardware store after the show. **Carl Andre** just wanted to have bricks that would go back to the construction company.

I don't think he would say that now!..

And **Sol LeWitt**, I gave him a one-man show in my gallery, his first one-man show — and he said that the work was wood, he said it should be used for firewood, that was a contradiction, so I thought to destroy value I would just put works as magazine pages. This was two years before there was such a thing as 'conceptual art', before art-language contact. I thought it would be disposable. One of my pieces, Side Effects of Common Drugs', it used to be a chart in a woman's magazine with the drugs women would take, would have side-effects and they would have to take other drugs, so it was a very optical chart.

"It also comes out of "Mothers Little Helper", the Rolling Stones song where the Rolling Stones said, they were accused of using drugs, but in fact housewives used more than they do..."

Dan Graham

SIDE EFFECTS / COMMON DRUGS
1966

offset on paper,
114,3 × 74,9 cm

What a drag it is getting old
"Kids are different today"
I hear ev'ry mother say
Mother needs something today to calm her down
And though she's not really ill
There's a little yellow pill
She goes running for the shelter of a mother's little helper
And it helps her on her way, gets her through her busy day

"Things are different today"
I hear ev'ry mother say
Cooking fresh food for a husband's just a drag
So she buys an instant cake and she burns her frozen steak
And goes running for the shelter of a mother's little helper
And two help her on her way, get her through her busy day

Doctor please, some more of these
Outside the door she took four more
What a drag it is getting old.

"Men just aren't the same today"
I hear ev'ry mother say
They just don't appreciate that you get tired
They're so hard to satisfy, You can tranquilize your mind
So go running for the shelter of a mother's little helper
And four help you through the night, help to minimize your plight

Doctor please, some more of these
Outside the door, she took four more
What a drag it is getting old

"Life's just much too hard today,"
I hear ev'ry mother say
The pursuit of happiness just seems a bore
And if you take more of those, you will get an overdose
No more running for the shelter of a mother's little helper
They just helped you on your way,
through your busy dying day

The Rolling Stones:

Mothers Little Helper
Jagger/Richards
LP "Aftermath" 1966

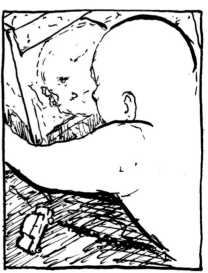

II.

WATER in DIGBETH

II/1 THROUGH THE GATES OF REFLECTION

But you see, my work, since it involves reflectiveness in relationship with transparency, water is also reflective and transparent at the same time and here we have canals, which reflect the sky and also have a kind of flow to them..

and my work is more baroque than it is minimal art, it changes in time, as you walk around it you see imagery of your body and other people's bodies moving in relation to each other and also in relationship to the sky...

This project, which was never realized, had a lot to do with the corporate atriums and the large corporate buildings in the centre of the city, where in the 80's they always had oversized mirrored columns. A good example is in this article I wrote for *Building Design* - this is a corporate atrium which is landscaped inside, and you can see this huge reflective column; so I thought here that this could be in a kind of corporate plaza, and the **body** is inside the **column**. and you can see people on either side. and as you move, you see anamorphic distortions of your body, and as you go under here. this is a little like a baroque church ceiling, except you're seeing the real sky and yourself distorted rather than angels. And the way the two-way-mirror-pieces work is very different than **corporate** buildings, where they're one-way mirror, they're reflected on the outside, and they're transparent on the inside looking outside. And on the outside the buildings look like the sky. its kind of a corporate alibi, because in the Jimmy Carter period, Jimmy Carter said the corporations were destroying the environment. so what the corporate office buildings did, and the bank building**s**, is, they used two-way mirror glass reflecting the sky, so the corporation identified themselves with the **sky**. also it cut down air-conditioning costs because the two-way mirror reflected the light on the outside, cutting down inside air-conditioning

Portal Model, 1997

* Dan Graham wrote an article on American corporate interiors for "Building Design" 1988. The article was shown on large photocopies at Eastside Projects.
'Odysseys in Space', in: Building Design, 1988, p. 38-43, D.Graham/R.Hurst

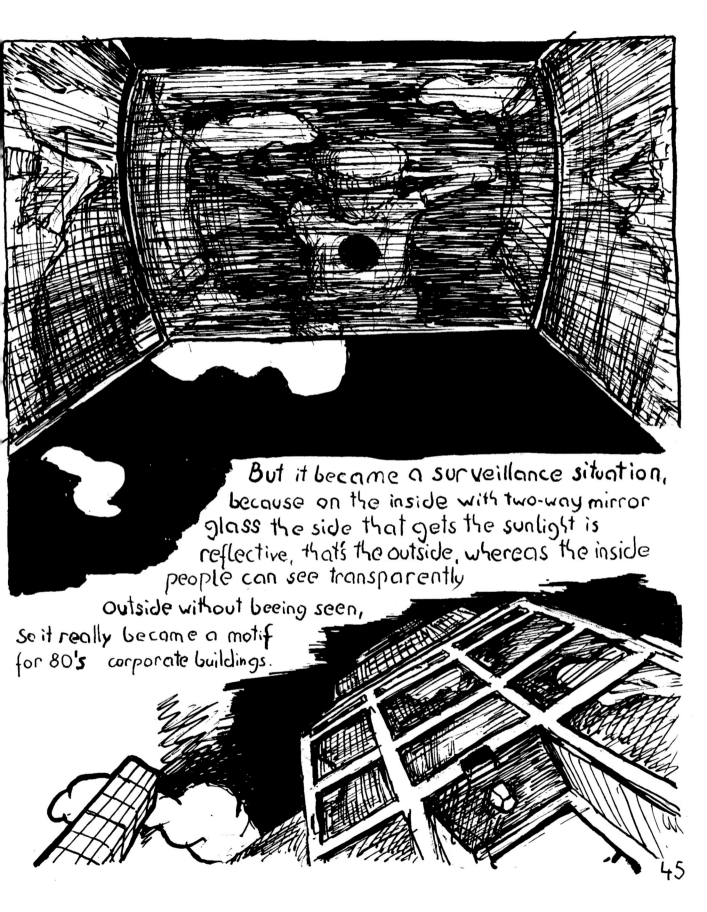

so there is a shift of light... and different from minimal art this work takes place in time as you walk around it, and also as the sky changes... and I think...

...I use water because it's another reflective element...

This is what I..

...I've never thought about that... that if water...
people love to look out across water...
and they love that reflection
I have never really pinned down why... but
and from what you were saying yesterday —
that idea of being able to understand the space
between other people's gazes and viewpoints... I am just
trying to imagine what it is... is it a self-learning that people are doing
when they are part of that process, are they, I don't know... is there
a heightened self-awareness or...

No, I don't think so at all...

...Well it's as you put it...
it really comes from when I was 14
and I read Jean Paul Sartre's 'Being and Nothingness'
and the mirror-stage that Lacan picked up on
is actually described in Being and Nothingness
Sartre said, the child has a fragile sense of
himself as an ego, when he sees somebody
who is gazing at him at the same time
and I think you get that in Mies van der Rohe's Barcelona Pavilion

1929, reconstructed 1986

48

you see a fleeting image of yourself and other people seeing themself and of the material at the same time. The pavilion form really goes back to the follies of the baroque garden, or the gazebos in the 19th century garden, and finally temporary exhibition buildings like the Barcelona Pavilion. And I also relate it urbanistically to the city where you have bus shelters and telephone booths, so it's kind of an anonymous form that's halfway between art and architecture... I think this is why I was attracted to the old train station because it's kind of a waiting room situation, right...

Curzon Station (1838)

Railway station in Birmingham. Closed in 1966. Worlds oldest piece of monumental railway architecture. (by Philip Hardwick)

So, Dan, each of these different things, because you mentioned quite a lot of different types of pavillions and structures, I just wanted to go back to the reflecting pool, because the reflecting pool, historically, is that something to do with the idea of the gods, that the Greek gods would look through a pool and be able to see the mortals below, and some kind of mythical...

I am starving

yeah, I think it might have been a portal, it was meant to be godlike, a link, a screen between the gods and the mortals

Wasn't the reflecting pool a portal?

Because Orphée looks at the mirror in order to speak to the dead, right? so it's a kind of portal

I guess... well Cocteau picks up on that aspect

50

You told me something about the connection between the portal and the new model that we realized for the show — in some way, you said that the portal has something to do with the idea of the column that you studied and the model for Birmingham...

There is one project that I made a sketch for when I saw the train station and it's the one over there... But there is no relationship to the Portal Model

How long is that from the Portal Model? About 5 or 10 years ago?

Maybe about eight years ago... I thought this would be very good near the old train station, the **Curzon**, which has these big neoclassical columns because this side [of the pavilion] is actually a sliding door, you can enter through here. What I also liked about that area was my work is very involved with the sky itself, so this is an open area and as the sun shifts position and clouds shift, that's reflected here; and also it's very child friendly, because on the inside small boys can see themselves anamorphically enlarged like **superman**, whereas somewhat overweight woman see themselves as thin on this side, and of course my work is about the relation between people looking at each other on either side.

This is where it comes from. Sartre and Lacan's mirror stage and as you walk around, you see yourself anamorphically moving, as you walk, and also the sky changes, and as the sky changes, in terms of the clouds in the sky, the relations between what side is more transparent and which is more reflective is constantly shifting

ELSEWHERE...

And then, Japanese architects like **Itsuko Hasegawa** and **Shinohara** started using perforated metal

it's become picked up by a lot of architects. Western architects like **Jean Nouvel** and **Steven Holl** and I am using the division between the two parts of the pavilion, using perforated metal here...

well let me show you some of the water things, because we are talking about...

...water pieces...

They are actually very specific to suburban and urban situations I have experienced... I spent some time in Australia, I had an Australian girlfriend, and the first thing I noticed in Australia is people who have middle-income houses always have a fishpond and a swimming pool, but they are not put together. So I was reading at the airport this swimming pool magazines, and I came up with this idea - a combination of a fishpond and a swimming pool.

SWIMMING POOL/FISHPOND Model, 1997

It cant be that big, because the water pressure is so enormous, it would collapse. So with an engineer I worked out the fact that you can have distorting two-way mirror glass below the water, it's called thermal, and above it's just safety glass. It wouldnt be this severe, this is exaggerated, the ramp, but I like the fact that you get anamorphic distortions where the fish are enlarged here, they become very large in fact you can put your hand inside and see what happens.

like this...

"Well no, it was based on the Hudson River School, th Hudson River itself, and also on the environment of the new American continent. And from an European point of view you call it _the sublime_, so it was an **AMERICAN SUBLIME**... ...in a way..."

"Why is the sky bigger in America than Europe?"

"It was unpopulated than..."

"It's a large country, I don't know, I never understood that, but it is, it's much, much vaster..."

"And what Caspar David Friedrich did, was he had people meditating in front of the sky, so it was a very civilised situation, whereas in America it was just the sky itself, and I think **Flavin** takes directly from that. Ed Rusha said in an interview that he was deeply influenced by Bierstadt - Bierstadt was originally Swiss, before he came to America..."

Albert Bierstadt, Yosemite Valley, 1868, Oil on Canvas.

II/2 TIMESLUDGE

The music that influenced me was the element of time, because I think in the middle 60ies everybody wanted things to be instantaneous present time, that was what the dogma was. **Lawrence Weiner** still says he wants his work to put people in contact with absolute present time, and instantaneous present time, but I think, I was critiquing that, because the work I was looking at, had a lot to do with movement and time, and also the feeling of the body, as you perceive yourself as a spectator, in a time-based situation. And I think a lot of musik, like **La Monte Young's** music, you get a feeling of the sound emanating from the walls of the architecture and also from inside your brain – and the kind of brain-time, extended present time as a **brain time**... **it's very much the experience of marijuana**... at that time period...

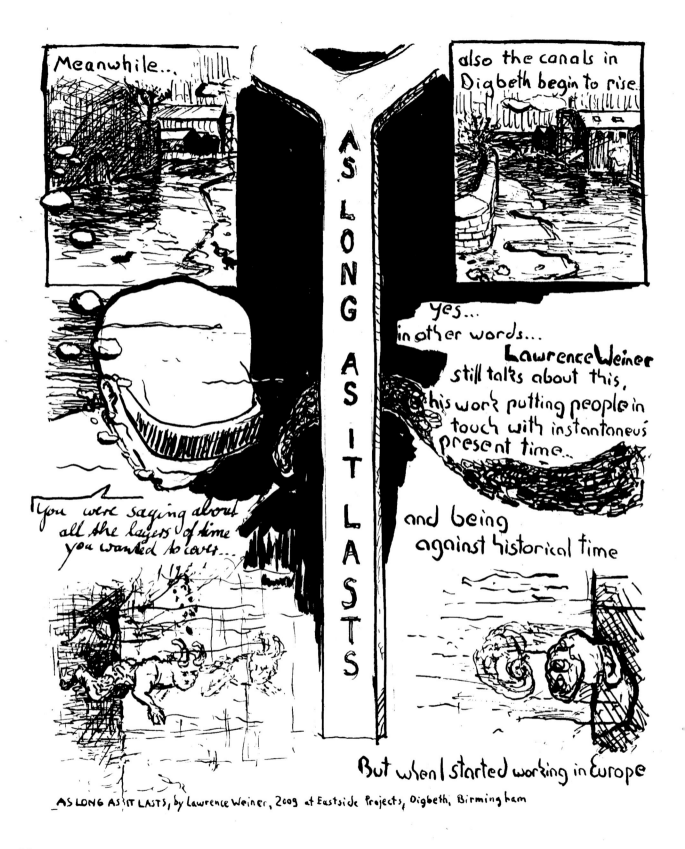

...as well as the marijuana and music influence...

I realized, the gardens that I was working in had an overlay of different historical periods of gardens

when you go to Europe, its an overlay of different time periods sometimes...

Yeah simultaneously, right — they're always there.

and at Eastside Projects...

Ah, we are intrested, in whether the gallery can do that as well -- whether the gallery can have these simultaneous times

like those gardens

bloody canals

THE WATER DARKENS WE MUST BE GETTING CLOSER...

TO SOMETHING...

Well I think the person you should talk to about this is **T. J. Clark** who now lives in England. He's come back to England—his wife, his partner who works for the Tate Modern, and his next project...

you read the Poussin book, right? the amazing book about Poussin's paintings that T.J. Clark wrote, called...

I read a part of the constructivist one, about El Lissitzky

No, not El Lissitzky it was called **Farewell to an Idea**

it was a very big book

T.J. Clark
1943
Art historian, writer
1999: Farewell to an Idea
Episodes from a History of Modernism
2006 The Sight of Death
An experiment in Art Writing
This book revolves around two paintings by Nicolas Poussin:
Landscape with a calm (1651)
Landscape with a man killed by a snake (1648)

'Pleasure Island' is floating!!!

it transforms..

SPLASH!

II/3 STAR SPECKLED ORBIT

But also my culture, because I began in magazines, was media culture, and I have to say, the biggest influences on American art in the 60ies were **Jean-Luc Godard's** early films; the New Novel, of not Robbe-Grillet, who I didn't like very much, but **Michel Butor**, who did a book about a city a little like Birmingham, getting lost in a Northern industrial English city, and the city was like a labyrinth and he was trying to figure it out.

Butor has a huge influence not only on my writing, but also **Sol Lewitt and Aldo Rossi**.

Michel Butor 1926- was part of the Nouveau Roman (New Novel) movement until 1960. The book Dan refers to, is L'emploi du temps, 1956 (Passing time)

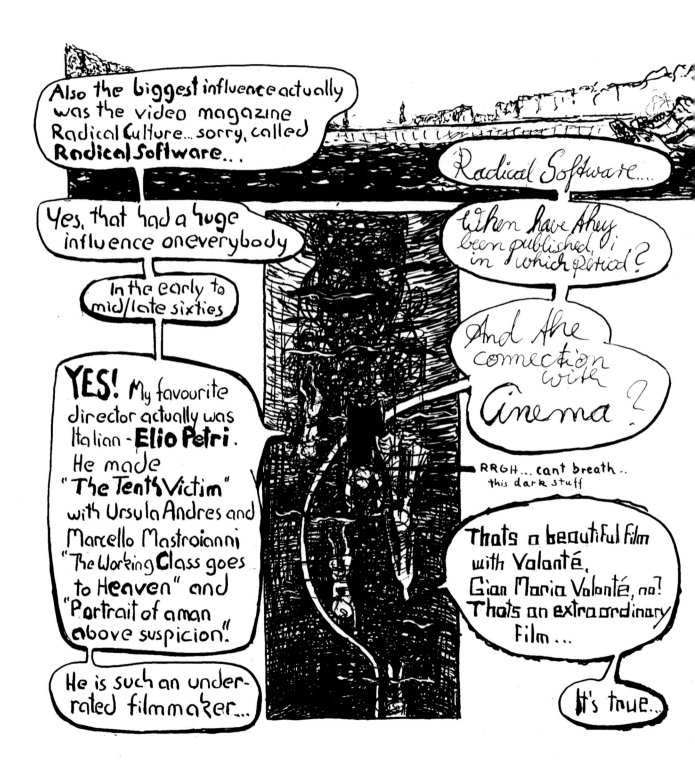

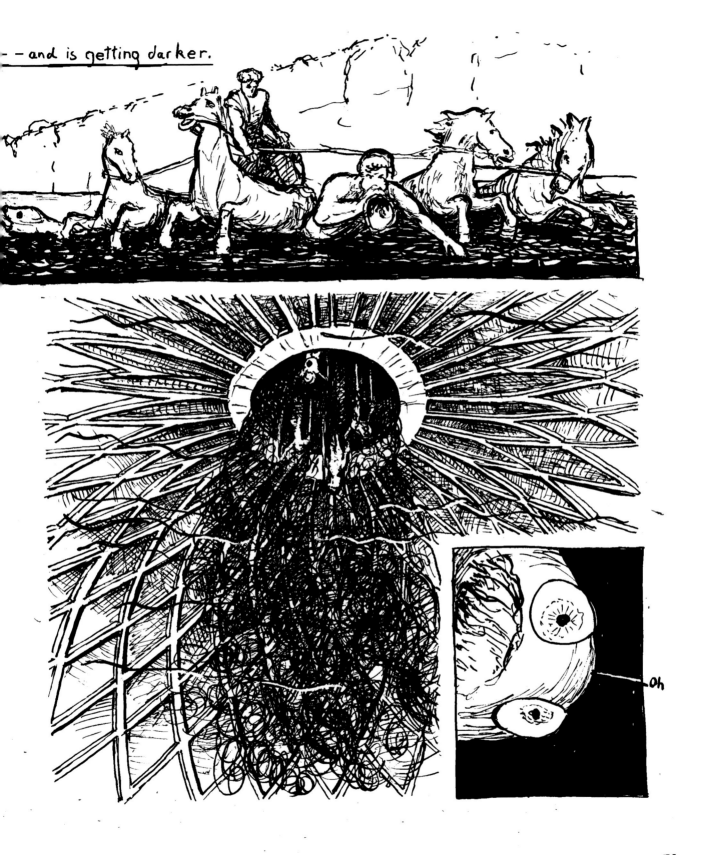

"I don't talk to critics

the critics have no interest in my work anyway"

Frank Gillette became Raindance first president

a like-minded group of videographers and others founded in 1969

RAINDANCE CORPORATION
"an alternative culture think-tank"

publisher of

RADICAL SOFTWARE — THE ALTERNATE TELEVISION MOVEMENT — NUMBER 1 — 1970

RADICAL SOFTWARE VIDEO Journal
11 issues published 1970-1974

Founders and first editors of Radical Software

Phyllis Gershunny
Beryl Korot

Frank Gillette loaned Paul Ryan video equipment in spring 1968 — very rare stuff at the time

all issues are now online www.radicalsoftware.org

Cybernetics of the Sacred
published 1974
Predates the cyberpunk ethic, taking as subject the video camera

"a supremely bad piece of drivel about videotape and knots and "cybernetic guerilla warfare" making no sense whatsoever"
a comment found somewhere in the web...
Well I personally LOVED it...

Paul Ryan — born 1943, writer, video artist, theoretician

Teaches at The New School, N.Y. as McLuhan Fellow

II/4 EMULATIONAL TIMING

Walter Benjamin said a lot of things that are fashionable are 'Neo'. Neo 30's, neo 50's. And he said that destroys the just past. So for real history to exist, you have to have the just past related to the present. What people were doing was, they didn't like the 80s so they went back to the neo 60s. Like **Jorge Pardo** or **Buckminster Fuller**. So what I wanted to do was introduce the history of the 70s and 80s to keep it related to present time and history. Benjamin talked about that often, because he was against historicism. **Historicism** means you fantasise another time period from the past.

What would we do here in Digbeth then?

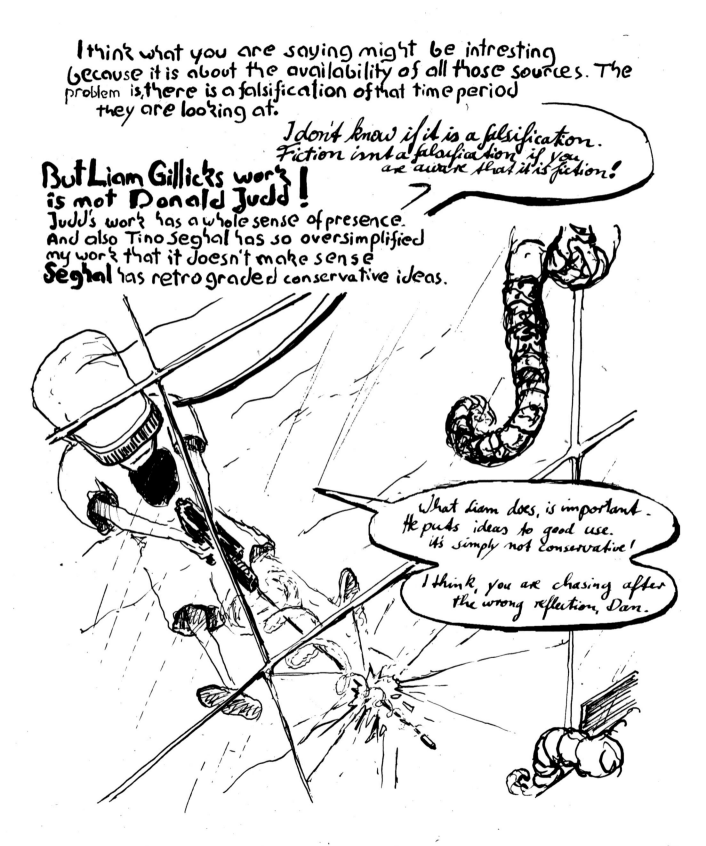

III.
ET
IN
ARCADIA
EGO

Wilhelm Reich was criticizing conservativeness of his first teacher Freud, because Freud was very pessimistic and said civilisation will win out, and he believed sexuality was very important, but he saw it as a kind of conservative tendency. Wilhelm Reich was actually Marxist in the beginning, he did a Marxist critique of Freud and in the end he believed in liberating the body sexually whereas Freud, I think, was pretty much a conservative theoretican.

And then, the moment in 1968 which is that?

That comes from American hippy culture and Marcuse

But is that liberating the body?

That was coming from Marcuse's writing pretty much, he was the biggest influence on 68 culture

Yeah, the idea to go beyond traditional structure of family organization

It was **ANTI-OEDIPUS** you're exactly right, Maurizio. As a fellow traveller-hippy I was influenced by these ideas, but then I became a fellow traveller punk.

"No, what happened with hippies was people like Jerry Garcia, hippies became entrepreneurs and businessmen - entrepreneurs.

and I guess my position all along was anti-corporate culture

Americans really despise corporations
Americans have always hated corporations

How come, Dan there are so many of them that are American? So many Americans work for them...

Well, they're not American, they're multi-national, there's Shell - you know a lot of American corporations are owned by Canadians, it's become a multi-national situation."

In Front of Eastside Projects

PLEASURE ISLAND

"So what do you think is the role of a model in relationship to the real thing and to the world outside?"

"When I show these models, I usually show the videotape of the actual piece in front of it, so you have an overall view. But the first models I did were not like this at all, they were vernacular, they were very simple vernacular, and I did them for the Museum of Modern Art show I did in 1978. Mark Francis was the curator then

...and the ones that were halfway between sculpture and pavilions became propaganda for actual pavilions being built and the other ones Alterations to a Suburban House; Clinic and Video Projection Outside Home - were fantasy situations in suburbia."

after "Clinic for a Suburban Site" model, 1978

A temporary clinic had been set up for the victims of the flood. We went in.
The guards mission was accomplished. She vanished.

116

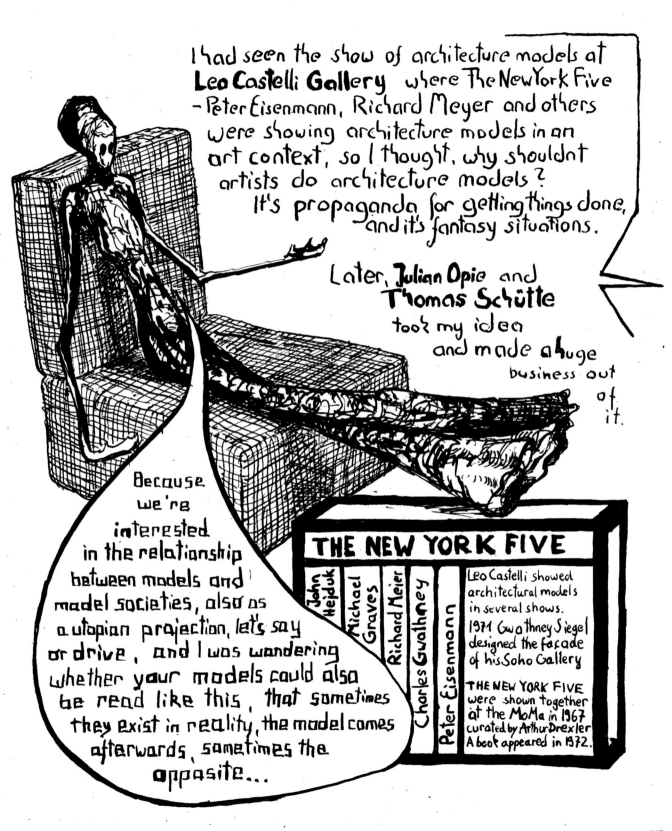

I AM AGAINST UTOPIA

Because it's a simplification. The 60's were not about utopia. The best book about utopia was the book that **Dolores Hayden** wrote: Seven American Utopias about the 19th century utopias.

Why?

Cool! But you could have a model that was anti-utopia, you could have a model that was attempting to go against the idea of heading towards utopia, that would still be...

Yah. Because the pieces by Dan they really interact with the space, with the place, with the landscape, and the changing situation around. So they are in real connection with the space, they are not utopian space, something that stays outside of the world.

Well, there is one connection I can make: **FOUCAULT** talked about **heterotopias;** so in a sense, they're taking dystopian buildings like corporate buildings, which are alienating, and making them into something like heterotopias in that sense there is a relationship to utopia, but not a planned utopia.

it's really against the dystopia of the corporate buildings. Of course, Foucault was talking about a heterogeneity of different perverse relationships you can have to the structure: in other words:

I think it allows play.

my sense of utopia — if there is any — comes from **Marcuse** — the idea of the polymorphous perversity of children's sexual experiences.

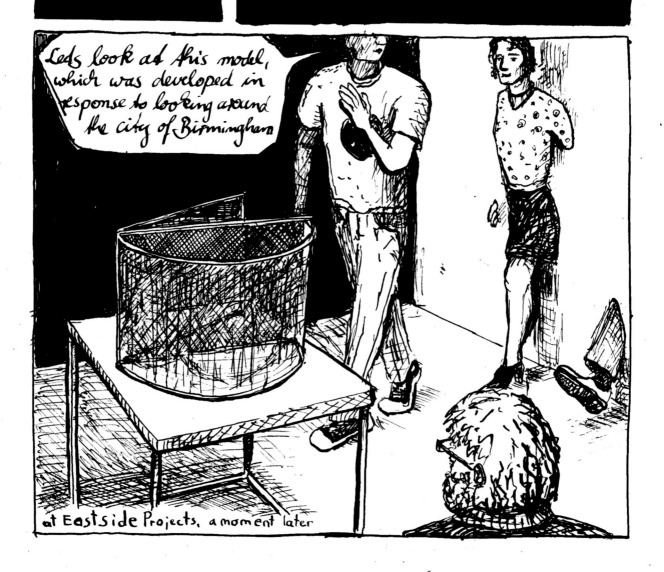

Dan looked at a number of places of interest, the Curzon Street Station... The model is called ~~Half Cylinder Perforated Metal Pavilion~~, Dan made as a response to the oversized neoclassical columns that are on the Curzon Street Station, and other civic aspects of the city. It's the idea of the pavilion echoing the architecture of the city. Dan, you want to say anything about the model form?

Oh yeah...

There are two discrete spaces... you can go in this this triangle - and there is a sliding door, so you can go in here...
My work works very well with the sky and its both, reflective and transparent.

And I want to undermine the corporate idea of the surveillance situation -
when you are inside, you can look outside and see everything without being seen.
My work is also different from minimal art, its very much about the spectator observing himself whilest being observed by other spectators on the other side of the two-way mirror.

"What's your feeling towards Birmingham and what do you generally think of the city?"

My feeling is it's one of the most interesting multicultural cities I've been to in England. I'm particularly interested in the 'rock' and roll' the Indian and South Asian residents do.

I was particularly struck by the **Bullring** which was the first urban shopping center. It seems to have great ambition to be as big - or bigger than Manchester, a city that was very important for me because of its rock music. Bands like **The Fall, Joy Division and The Buzzcocks**

It's a city that's a strange contrast of architecture from neo-Georgian to a kind of <u>industrial banal.</u>

Gavin Wade and I are curating your new project for Eastside Projects and the Curzon Street Station area in Birmingham, where Birmingham City University is planning a new building complex.

In your view, how is the city changing, and what is the relationship between the pavilions and the transformations of the cities you work in?

I like my work to reflect two different realities of the city: historical remnants, which have a lot to do with restoring the past; and not just historicism and what happens to the area that's been gentrified where there'll probably be parks as recreation situation for children, single mothers with children, and grandparents, who have to mind the children.

a mile away, at the canals

another mile away

The project I am thinking of relates to the neoclassical columns of the old train station and would bring into play a modern glass architecture in relationship to neoclassical ideas. This is a little bit like **Mies van der Rohes** interest in **Schinkel**.

I would say, that your projects have a lot to do with living space, defined by human relationships. I think, its very evident, for example, when we watch your video "Death by chocolate" (2005). You could say that the transformation of cities today is very closely related to gentrification. Does your work have some connection with this key issue?

The idea is to create a new social space in the middle of the very anonymous gentrification message and the public and the upper middle class housing projects that follow gentrification.

We were discussing with Gavin your next show in Birmingham at Eastside Projects, and we are planning to show some of your models and video work, they are quite relevant. Have you also had a discussion about connecting the space and show at Eastside Projects with your project at Curzon street station? could you tell me some of your ideas about that relationship?

At the moment I just think, people have to have the history of the past projects I've done, so they **can** have an inkling of what I am about to do in the near future.

after Nicolas Poussin "Landscape with a Calm" 1650, 97 × 131,5 cm. Getty museum, L.A.

But the work I'm going to do in the future will have nothing to do with the show it will have lots to do with the local site-specific conditions, that are still being developed right now, so the show is more the background for the people in the city, and who go to the university, to have an insight into the fact, that my work is basically about suburban shopping malls...

INDEX

Aldiss, Brian — 71ff, 88
André, Carl — 19, 112
Archigram — 26, 76
Asimov, Isaac — 71
Associated Architects — 24
Barcelona Pavilion — 48ff.
Beatles — 62
Benjamin, Walter — 94
Bullring — 11, 120
Buren, Daniel — 101
Butor, Michel — 70
Buzzcocks, The — 120
Castelli, Leo — 115
Chamberlain, John — 75, 88
Clark, T. J. — 68ff.
Clinic for a Suburban Site — 114 ff.
Cocteau, Jean — 50
Cook, Peter — 25
Curzon Station — 49, 122ff.
Death by Chocolate — 10, 123
de Quincey, Thomas — 63
Eisenmann, Peter — 115
Fall, The — 120
Fehn, Sverre — 31, 36, 38
Foucault, Michel — 117
Flavin, Dan — 16, 18, 42, 58
Fuller, Buckminster — 75, 94
Garcia, Jerry — 113

Gillick, Liam   97, 103
Godard, Jean-Luc   70
Half Cylinder Perforated Metal Pavilion   51ff., 119ff.
Hasegawa, Itsuko   52
Hatton, Brian   16
Hayden, Dolores   116
Holl, Steven   52
Hudson River School of Painting   42, 58
Huxley, Aldous   71
Huyghe, Pierre   98
Judd, Donald   14, 97, 113
Joy Division   120
Lacan, Jacques   37
Le Corbusier   14, 16
Lewitt, Sol   14, 18, 19, 70
Lubetkin, Berthold   14
Marcuse, Herbert   109ff.
Marijuana   61ff.
Matta-Clark, Gordon   98
Marx, Karl   112
Meyer, Richard   115
Minimal Art   13
Monk, Jonathan   97
Morison, Heather and Ivan   7
Mothers Little Helper   21
Nervi, Luigi   75ff.
Nouvel, Jean   52
Pardo, Jorge   94
Parreno, Philippe   98
Petri, Elio   72ff., 87ff.
Portal Model   52

Poussin, Nicolas — 40
Price, Cedric — 27, 28
Radical Software — 72ff.
Reich, Wilhelm — 109ff.
Rossi, Aldo — 70
Rusha, Ed — 58
Russian Constructivism — 16
Ryan, Paul — 75, 88, 89
Sartre, Jean-Paul — 48
Schinkel, Friedrich — 123
Science Fiction — 71ff.
Seghal, Tino — 98, 103
Side Effects of Common Drugs — 19, 20
Shinohara, Kazuo — 52
Specials, The — 121
Swimming Pool / Fishpond — 56ff.
Szeemann, Harald — 76
The New York Five — 115
Time — 64ff
Tiravanija, Rirkrit — 98
Troggs, The — 8
van der Rohe, Mies — 48, 123
Versailles — 46
Warhol, Andy — 23, 87
Weiner, Lawrence — 61, 66, 100
Whiteman, Walt — 112
Young, La Monte — 61

EP 13.1

© 2013 Henrik Schrat & Eastside Projects

ISBN 978-1-906753-26-9

Edited by Gavin Wade

Published by Eastside Projects after the occasion of:

Dan Graham: Models & Videos
Curated by Maurizio Bartolotti & Gavin Wade
Eastside Projects, Birmingham; 26. February - 16. April 2011

Dan Graham text from recordings made on 21-25 February 2011 by Eastside Projects as agreed and proofed with the artist.

This graphic novel is an artwork by Henrik Schrat commissioned by Eastside Projects.

Eastside Projects
Heath Mill Lane, 86, Birmingham, B9 4AR, UK
0121-771-1778, www.eastsideprojects.org, info@eastsideprojects.org

Eastside Projects is a not for profit company Limited by guarantee reg: 6402007, an Arts Council England National Portfolio Organisation in partnership with Birmingham City University, supported by Paul Hamlyn Foundation Breakthrough Fund.

Thank you to: Dan Graham, Mieko Meguro, Maurizio Bortolotti, Celine Condorelli, Joe Hollyoak, Samuel Rogers, Julia Gavin, Georgie Park, Alex Bailey, Franz Koenig and Beth Bramich.